Welcome to Inky Mandalas Mix

Volume 4 in the series

Forty-seven, creative, themed, single-sided illustrations to help lift you from your busy world into a feeling of calm and satisfaction.

From elephants, owls, mice with melted cheese, guitars and Russian dolls… to lace and paisley… every hand-drawn detail was created with a passion for art and with you –the colourist - in mind. The pages are designed to vary in intricacy to suit mood and ability, with border/background space for those who enjoy shading or adding their own twist. As an artist, I enjoy adding my own twist to designs in some way, and like to know there is space to do such.

The designs are single-sided, on paper #60 approx 90gsm to my knowledge. Adequate for my colouring needs with pens and pencil and the odd spot of acrylic paint for highlights, but I always suggest (and do myself) placing a blank sheet under your working page, to protect the illustration beneath from leak/bleed through of certain pens.

To view demos of me colouring designs from my books, please visit my Amazon author page, or my Facebook page, all can be found via my website, www.Helenclaireart.co.uk

I hope you enjoy the book as much as I did creating it for you!

Enjoy bringing the designs to life!

Copyright © 2015 Helen Elliston
All rights reserved.
ISBN: 1519622503
ISBN-13: 978-1519622501

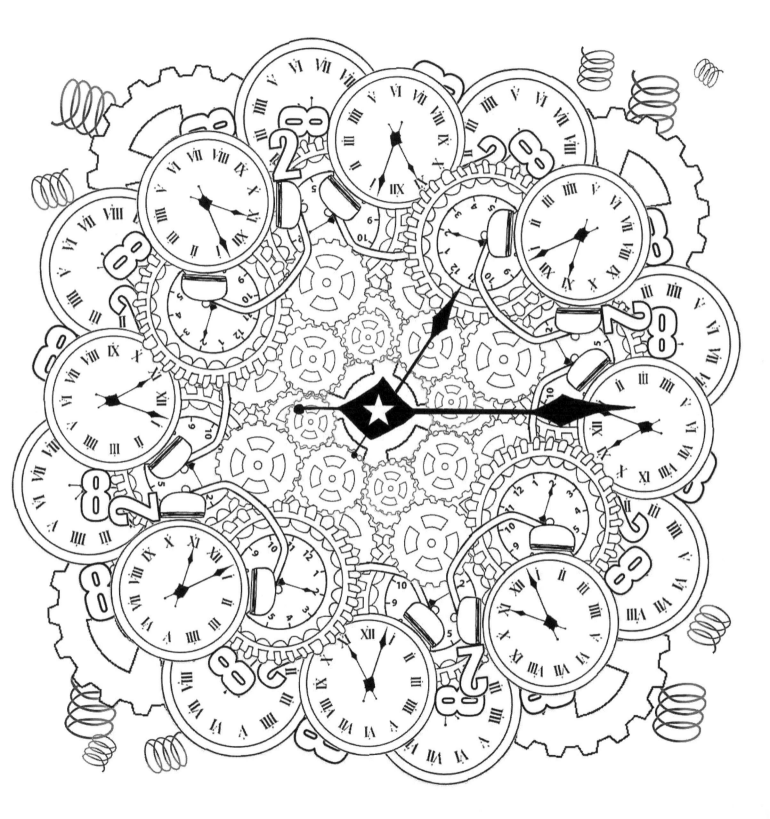

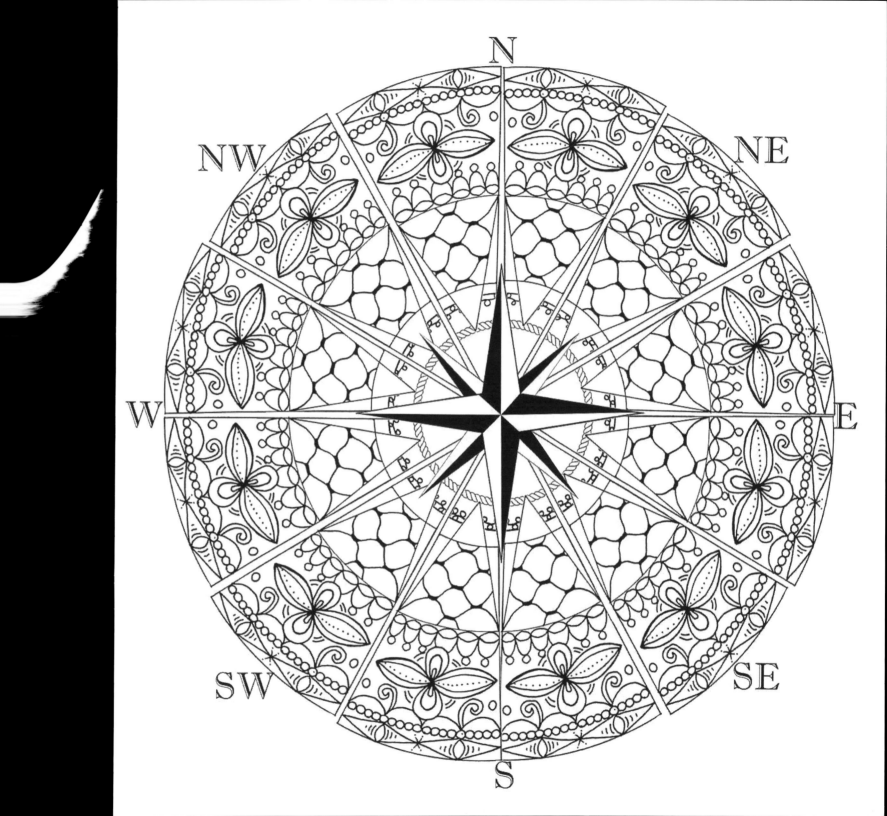

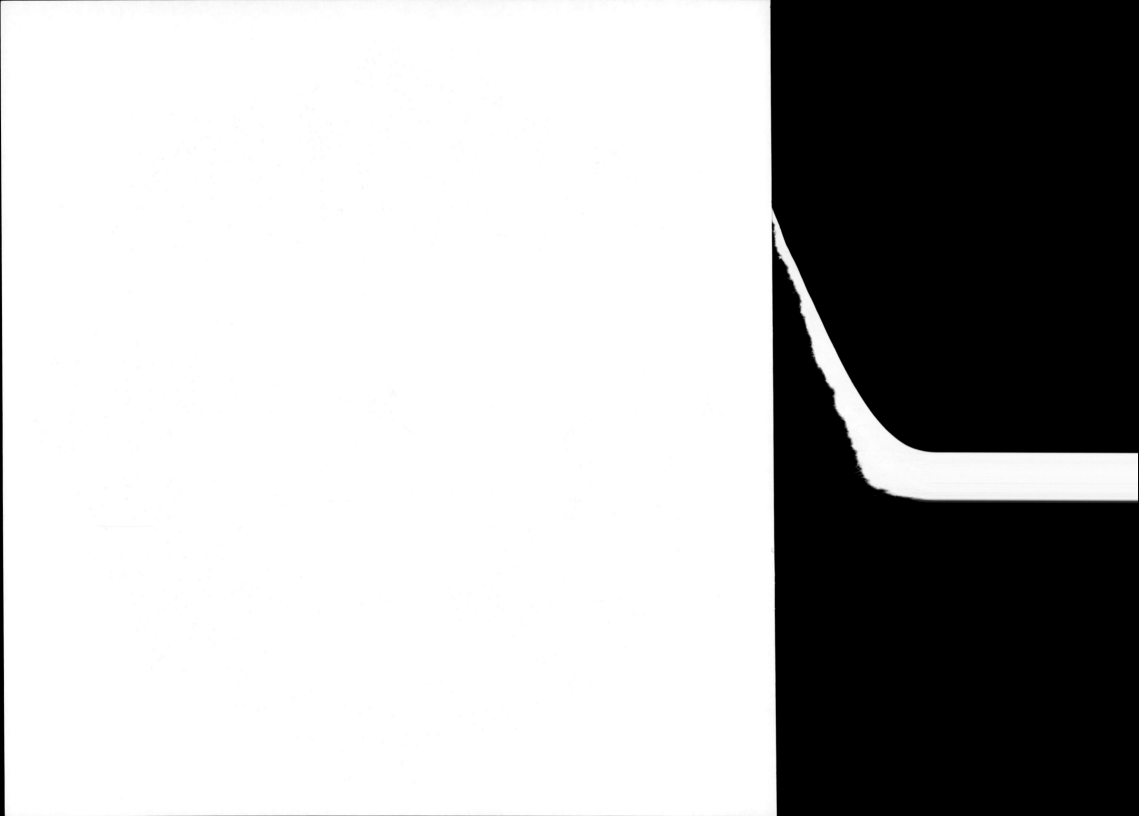

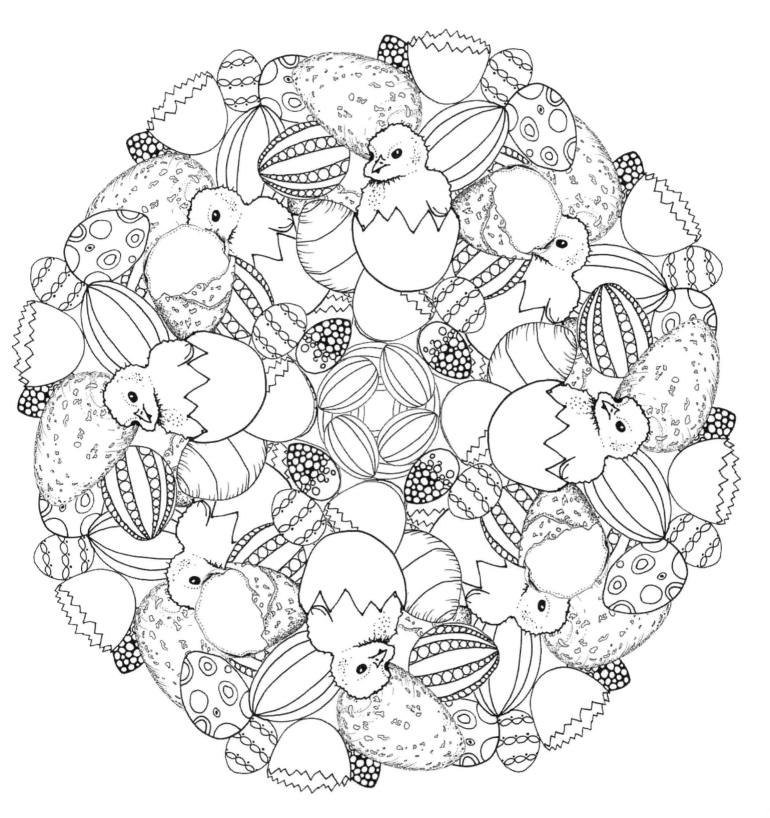

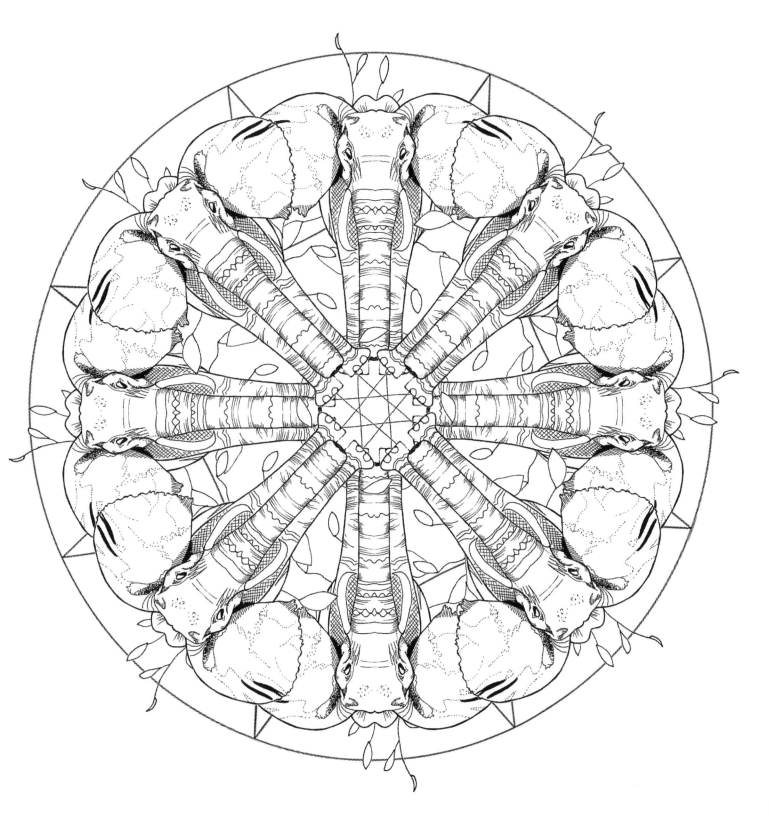

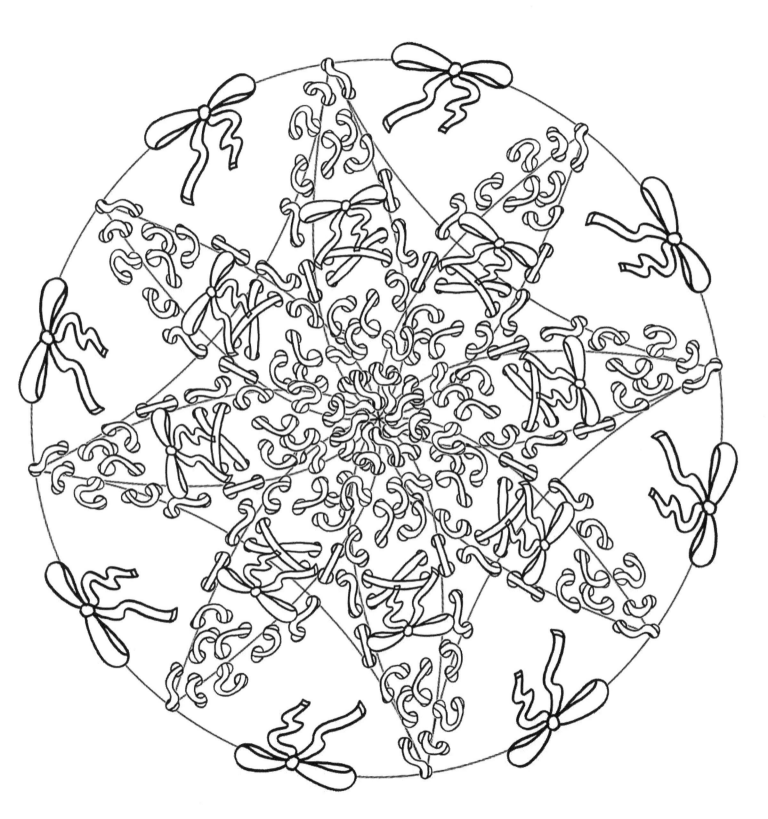

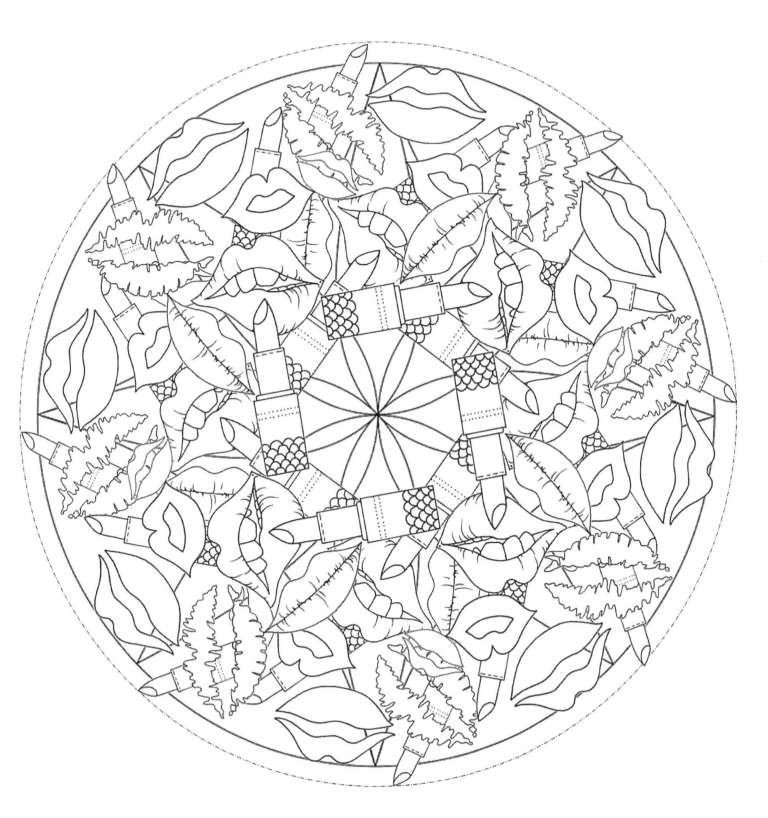

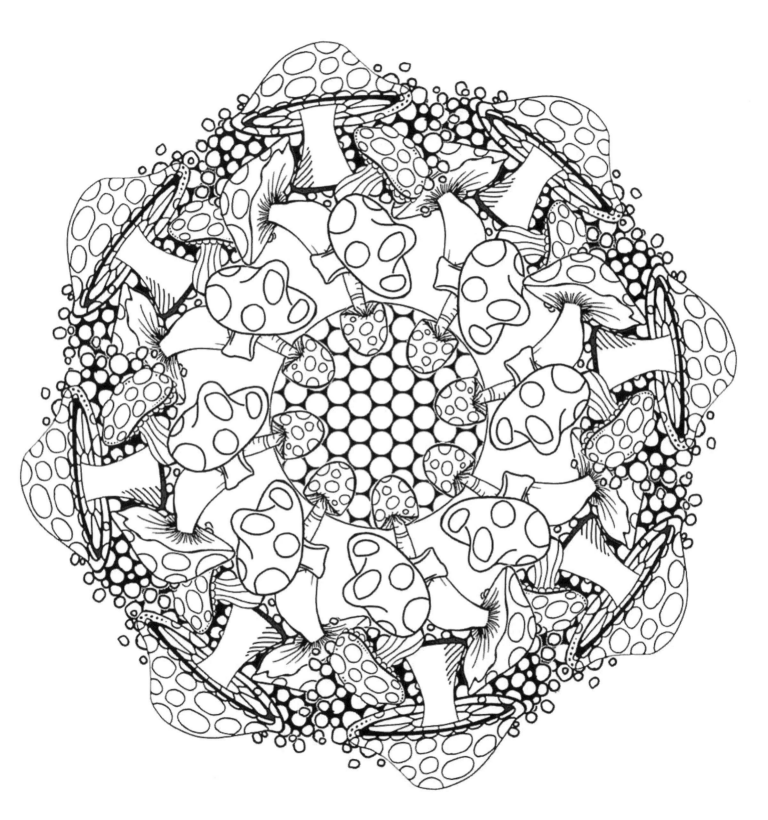

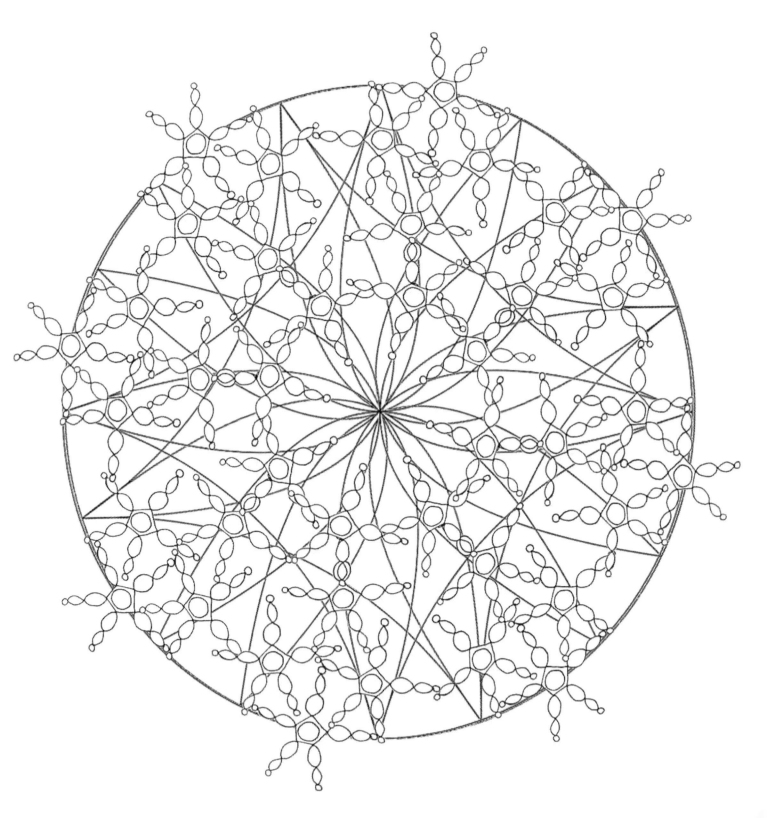

Printed in Great Britain
by Amazon.co.uk, Ltd.,
Marston Gate.